LAMORINDA

LAFAYETTE—MORAGA—ORINDA

ENE T. BONNYAY

DRUMGARTH LLC
MORAGA, CALIFORNIA

Library of Congress Catalog Card Number: 96-93726

ISBN: 0-9655360-1-7

Designed by Ene & Laszlo Bonnyay
Text and photographs by Ene T. Bonnyay

Published by Drumgarth LLC
Moraga, California

Printed by Kossuth Printing
Budapest, Hungary

BART mural detail of Joaquin Moraga Adobe,
California Historical Landmark
(By permission of the Orinda Historical Society)

Preface

LAMORINDA is the local name for the triangle formed by the three communities of LAfayette, MOraga and ORINDA. Nestled in the gently rolling hills and valleys of Contra Costa County, within a thirty- to forty-minute commute of San Francisco, the three towns share a common past.

The town of Moraga and parts of the cities of Orinda and Lafayette are located on land granted in 1835 by the Mexican government to Joaquin Moraga, the first Commandant of the Presidio of San Francisco, and his cousin, Juan Bernal. They received over 13,000 acres of the area known as Rancho Laguna de los Palos Colorados (Lake of the Redwoods Ranch). Parts of Orinda, and even more so Lafayette, sit on land from other land grants, but the Rancho Laguna is a shared geographic heritage.

Over the past century and a half since Joaquin Moraga built his adobe on the hills of what is now Orinda and claimed possession of the Rancho in 1841, the area of Lamorinda saw many squatters and settlers descend on it.

Agriculture and orchards (walnut and pear) flourished, cattle-ranchers and dairymen settled. Great land owners had varying visions for the future of the region, but finally after the 1950's a building boom was on its way as developers saw the possibility of a very desirable "suburbia" in the area's proximity to San Francisco, its great climate (air-conditioned by fog on the ridges) and geographic beauty. The separate towns were not incorporated until quite recently—Lafayette in 1968, Moraga in 1974, and Orinda in 1985. Fortunately Lamorinda resisted the temptation to succumb to the suburban growth and sprawl of many neighbors; the three towns fiercely fought building on the ridgeline of the magnificent hills, and they banned high buildings. With great determination they have tried to keep a balance of suburban sophistication and pride in vestiges of the rural past. Cattle and horse ranches still can be found here coexisting with family neighborhoods. Preserving open space and protecting wildlife are important concerns, as are education, art and culture. Lamorinda is, of course, home to Saint Mary's College of California and the California Shakespeare Festival. It is not unusual in Lamorinda to pass an artist painting a beautiful spring orchard, and a few miles down the same road to see a lonely, scruffy coyote on his way to a creek for a drink of water.

An interesting crossroad brings together past and present, rural and suburban, wild and sophisticated.

I have tried in the following photographs to capture this dichotomy—the towns are not treated separately, but as part of a whole, LAMORINDA.

Town Hall—home of Dramateurs—Lafayette

The Hacienda—Moraga

Community Center

Henson's Arabian Center—Lafayette

Henson's Arabian Center

Left and above: Spring
Right: Great Oak Ranch—Lafayette

Left, above & right: Theater Square—Orinda

Theater Square—Orinda

Sunset over Briones Reservoir—Orinda's neighbor

Top: Moraga Ranch
Bottom: Cafe Terzetto—Moraga

Rheem Valley—Moraga
Right: Pear orchard

View from Alta Mesa—Moraga

La Fiesta Square—Lafayette

Above: Statue of Lafayette by Way Side Inn—Lafayette
Right: El Diablo Forge—Lafayette
Far right: Lafayette reservoir

Above & right: Garrett Building—Lafayette
Far right: Colors of fall & goblins

Above: Orinda Theater
Right: Park Theater—Lafayette
Far right: Rheem Theater—Moraga

Orinda Theater
Right: Mustard

Moraga Country Club

Orinda Country Club

Lafayette Park Hotel

Mt. Diablo—Lafayette's neighbor

The grass is greener...

Saint Mary's College of California

Saint Mary's College of California

Saint Mary's College of California

Saint Mary's College of California

Saint Mary's College of California

Saint Mary's College of California

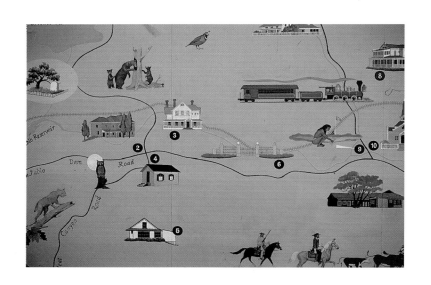

Above & right: BART mural—Orinda
(By permission of the Orinda Historical Society)

Lower right: BART station—Orinda

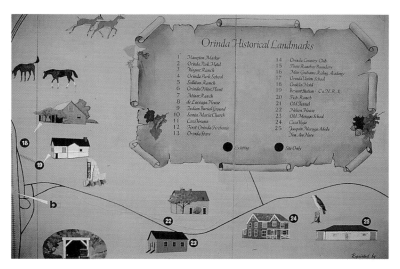

Casa Azul—Orinda

Santa Maria Church—Orinda

Bien Venida—de Laveaga home—Orinda
(Orinda Landmark)

Holy Shepherd Lutheran Church—Orinda

Sanders Ranch—Moraga
(also left)

Hills: Winter (above)
Summer (right)

Above: Third School House—Lafayette
(Now: Lafayette United Methodist Church)

Left: Moraga Barn

Above: Poppies—Moraga Commons

Left: St. Monica's Catholic Church—Moraga

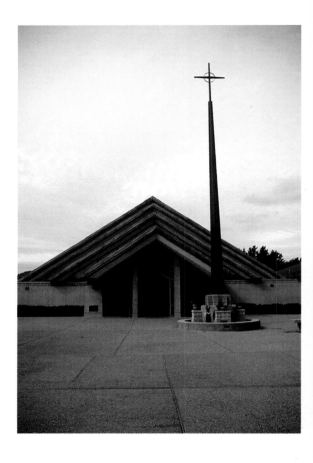

Moraga Valley Presbyterian Church

Right: Lafayette/Moraga Regional Trail

Lafayette—Orinda Presbyterian Church—Lafayette

The California Shakespeare Festival
Bruns Memorial Amphitheater—Orinda

Spring in the pear orchard

Right: Arts and crafts fairs

Artist—Susan McKenna List

Farmers' Market—Orinda

Farmers' Market—Orinda

Lemon harvest

Fourth of July—Moraga

The future of LAMORINDA